Copyright © 2020 by Marcysia Publishing

All rights reserved. This book or any portion thereof may not be reproduced or used in any manner whatsoever without the express written permission of the publisher except for the use of brief quotations in a book review.

NAUGHTY SECRETARY

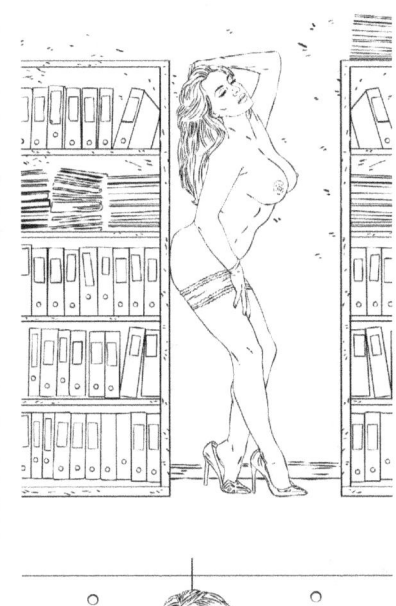
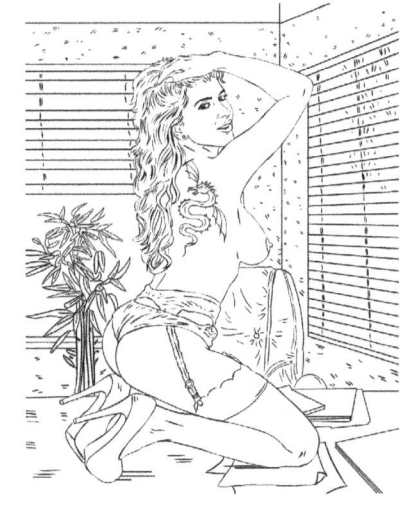
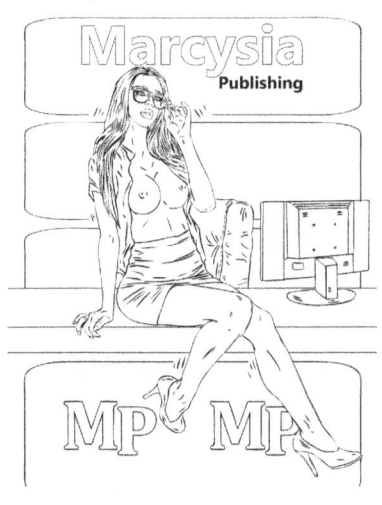
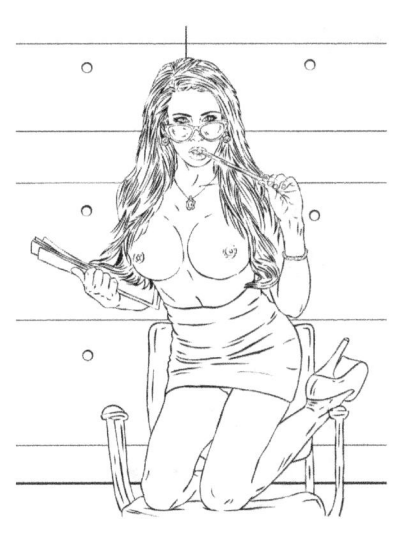
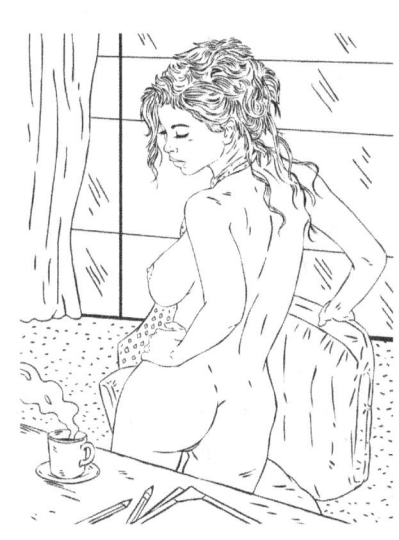
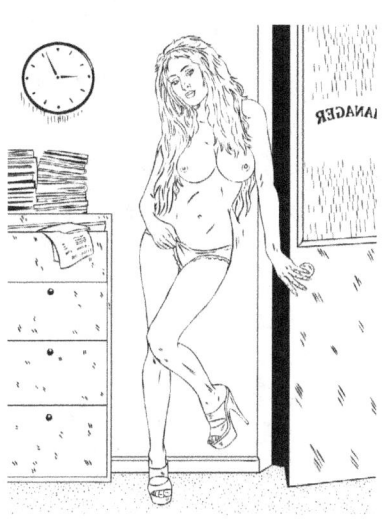
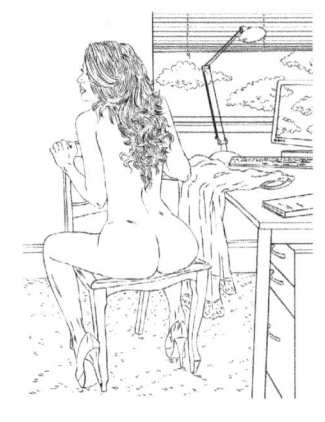
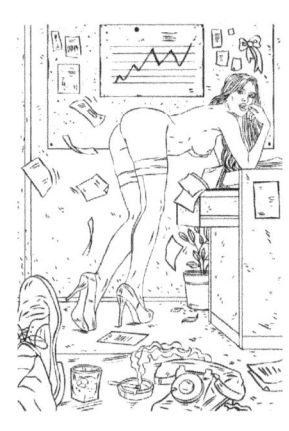
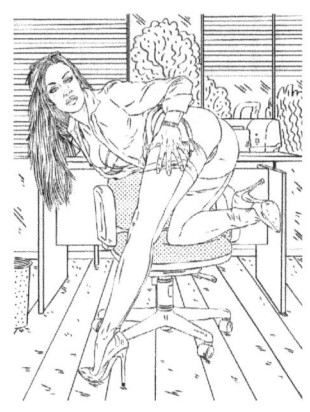
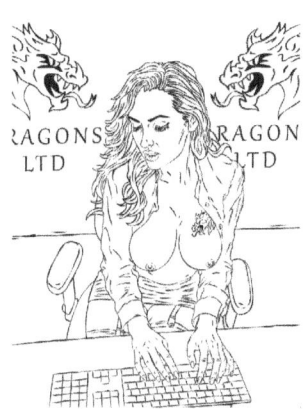

ADULT COLORING BOOK

Welcome to our slutty office. What a nice reception desk, isn´t it?

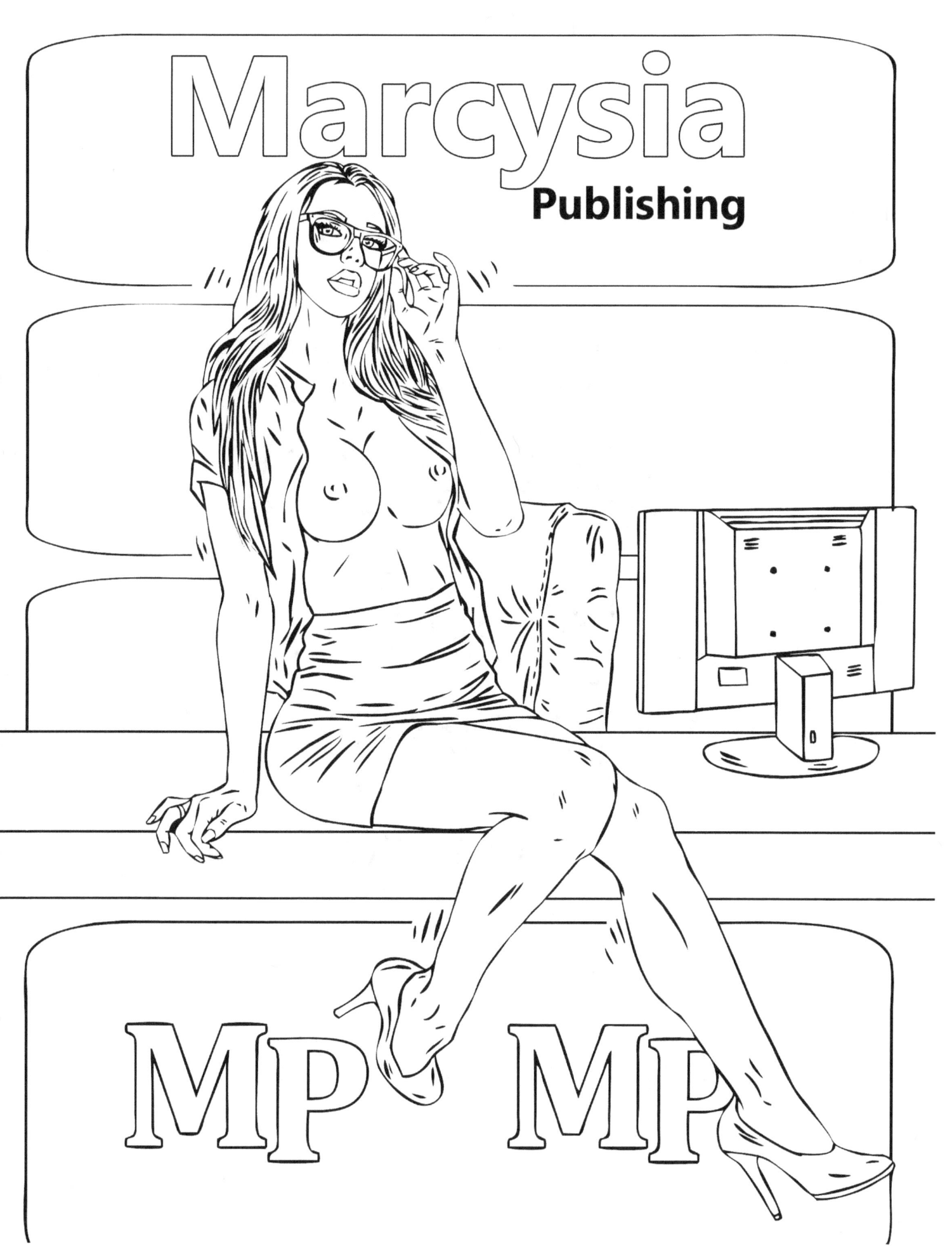

Meet our manager.
She's 3 B:
bichty
bossy
busy

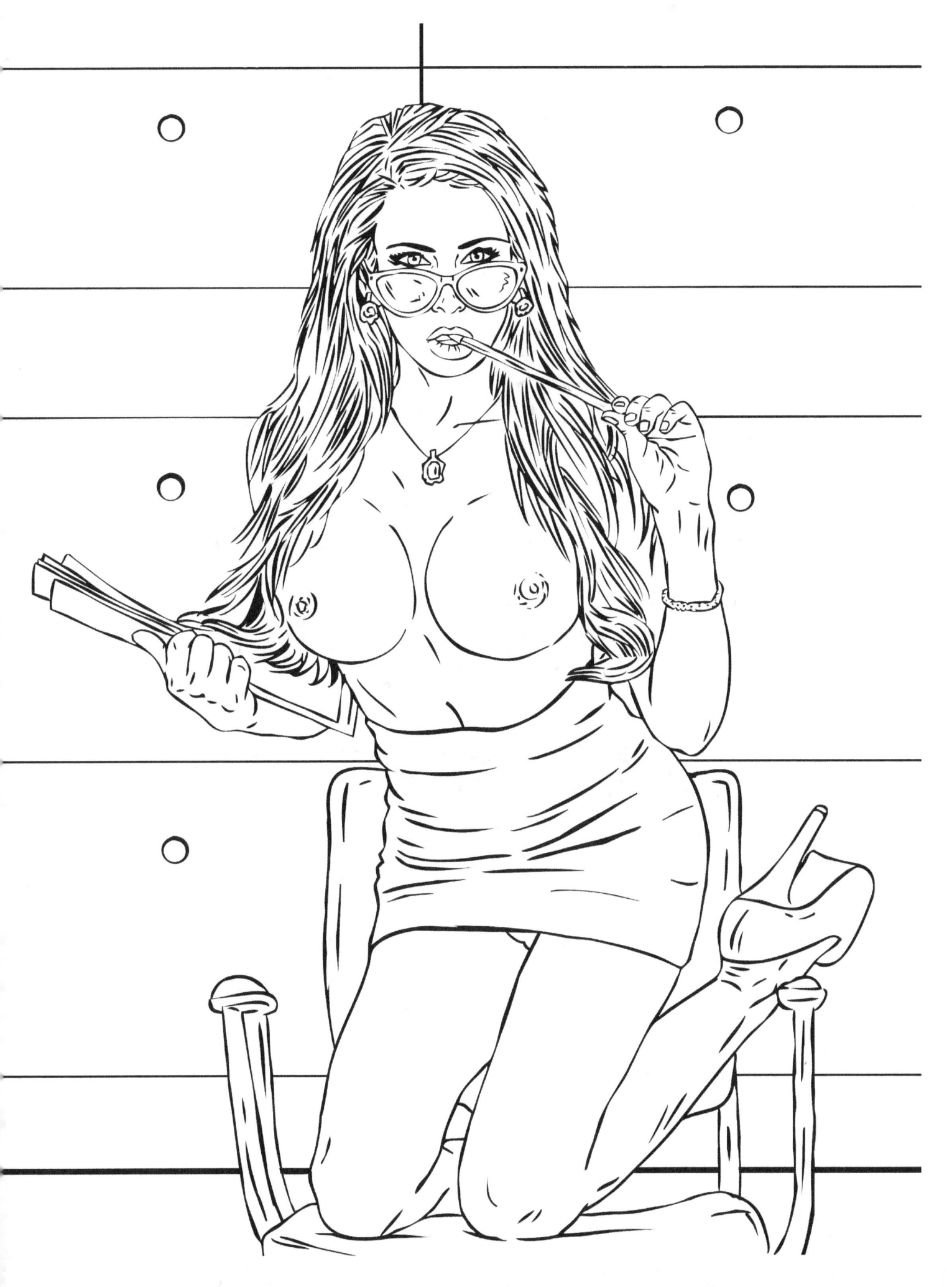

Emma, our accountant. Very shy but so meticulous!

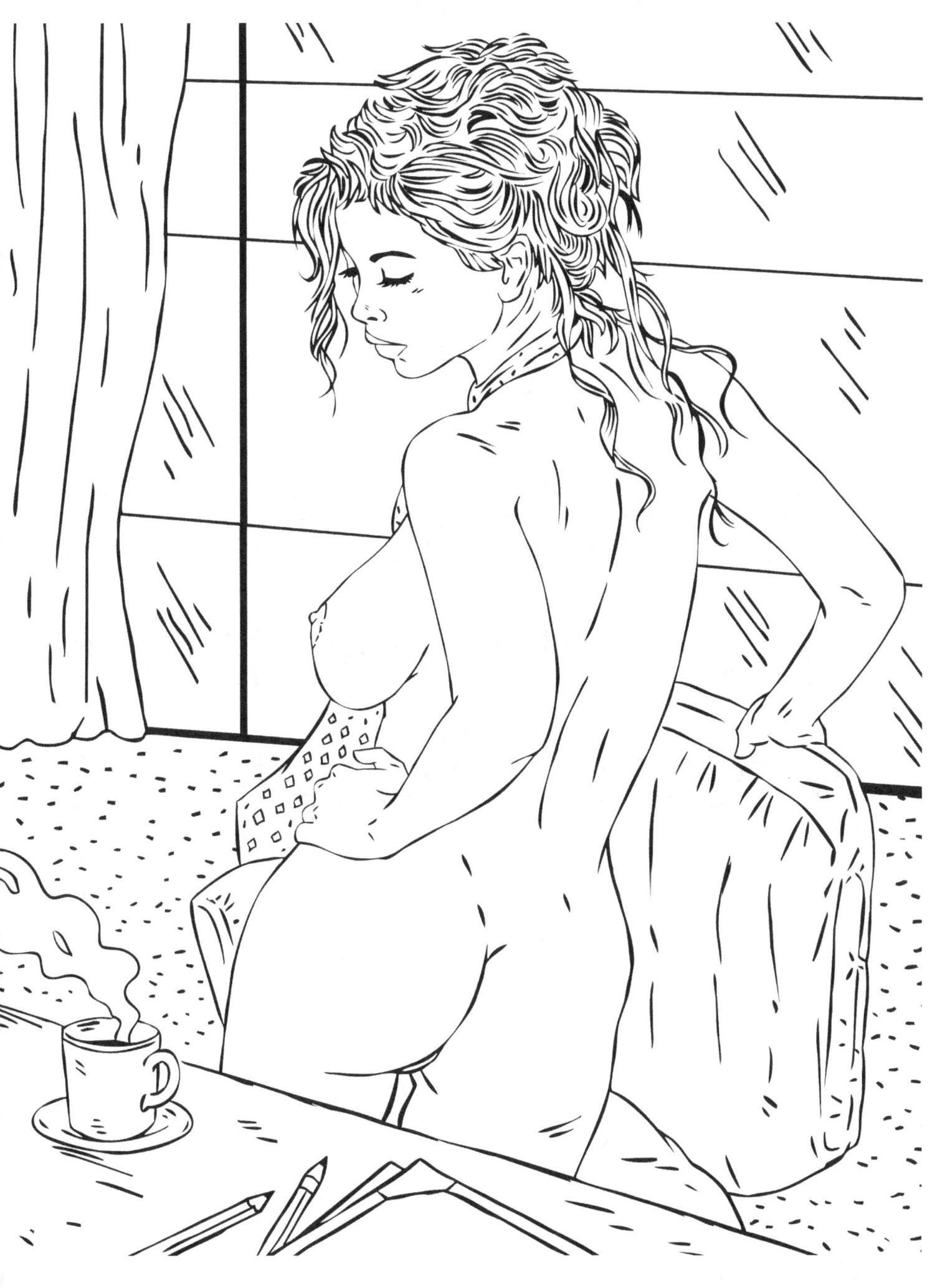

What does casual Friday look like in your office, huh?

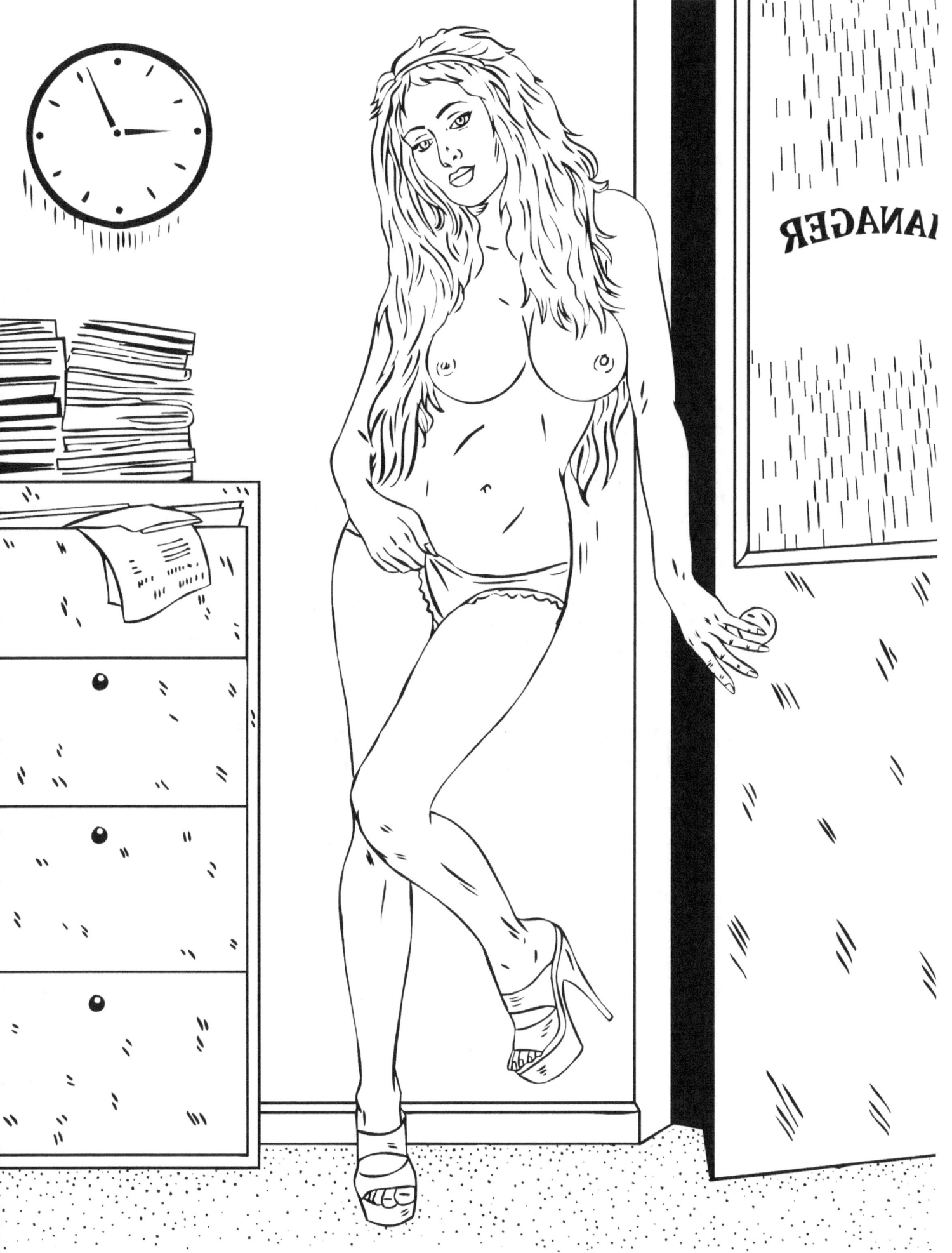

Meet Jessica.
Marketing,
obviously.

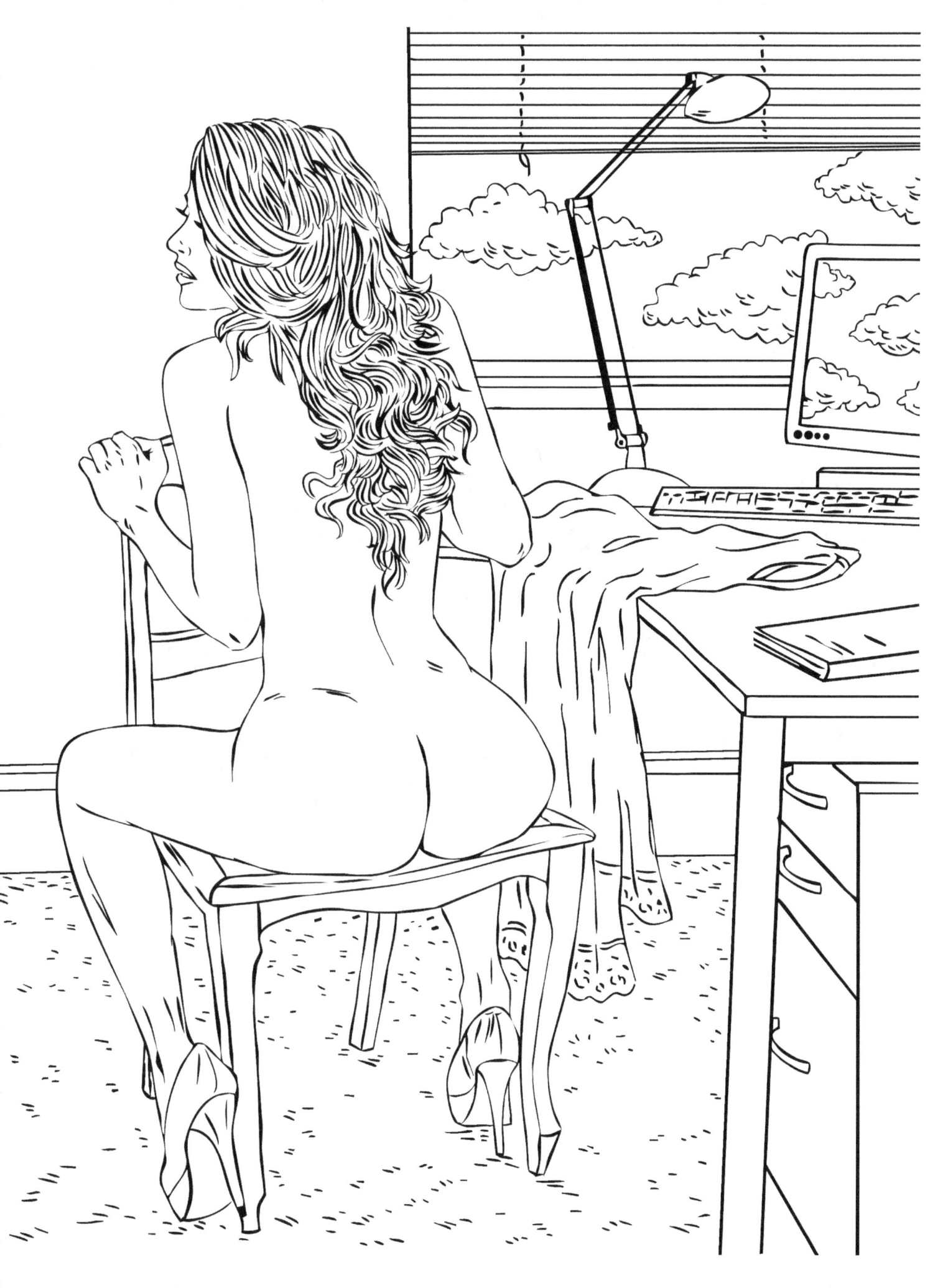

Sarah, the intern. Constantly looking for some papers...

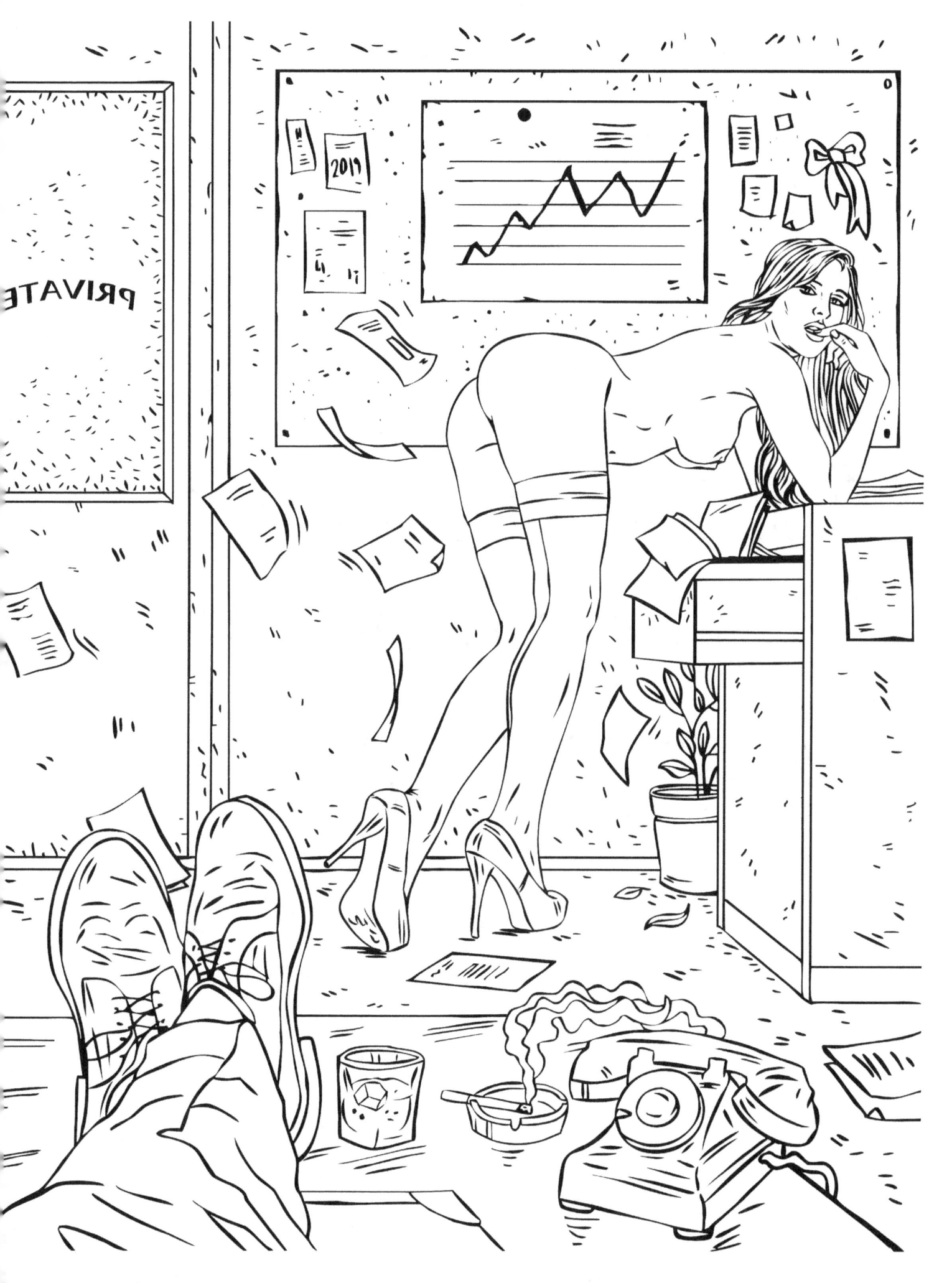

Taking good notes during a meeting is very important.

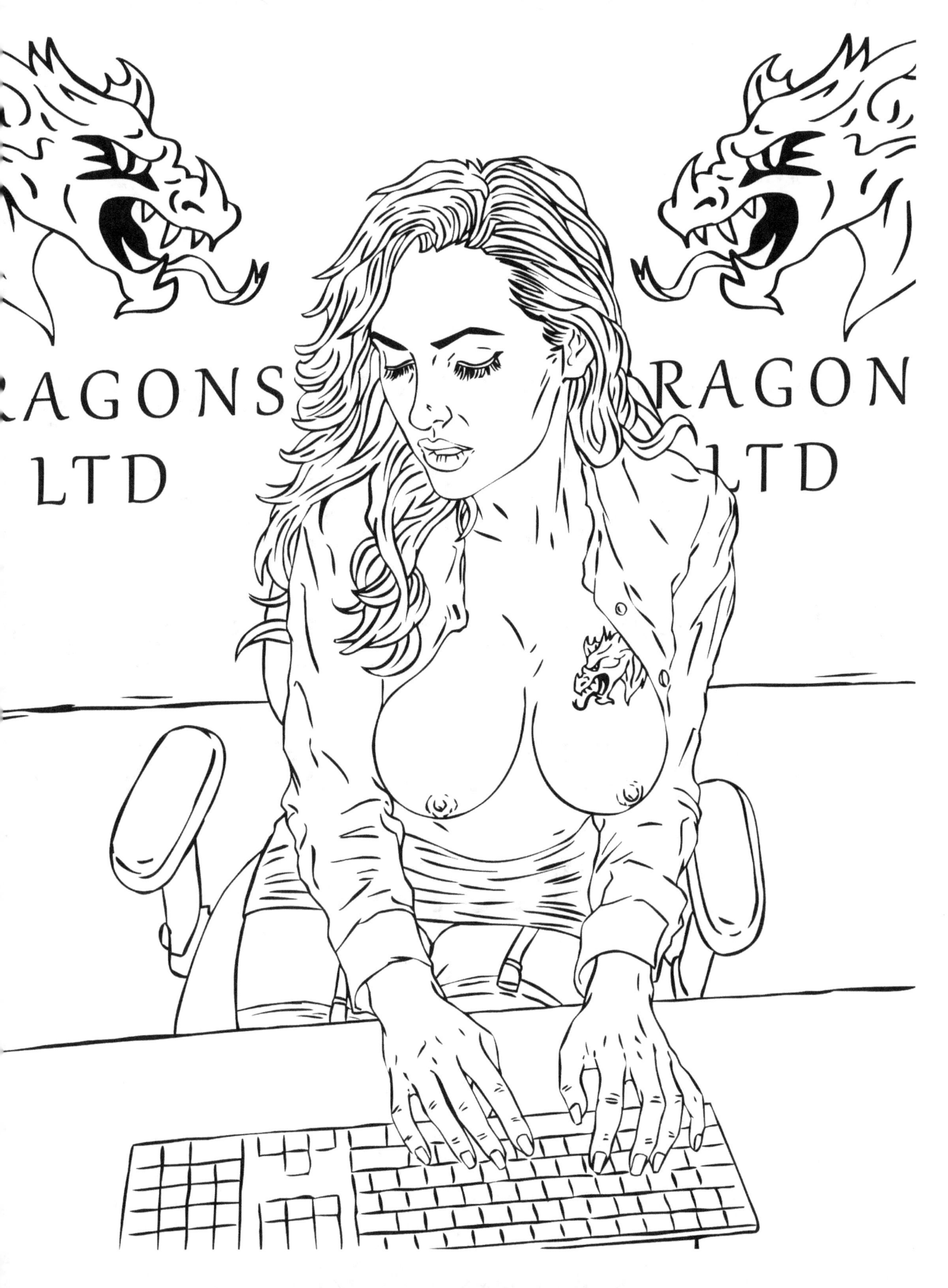

Don`t try to leave early today! We still have some things to delve into...

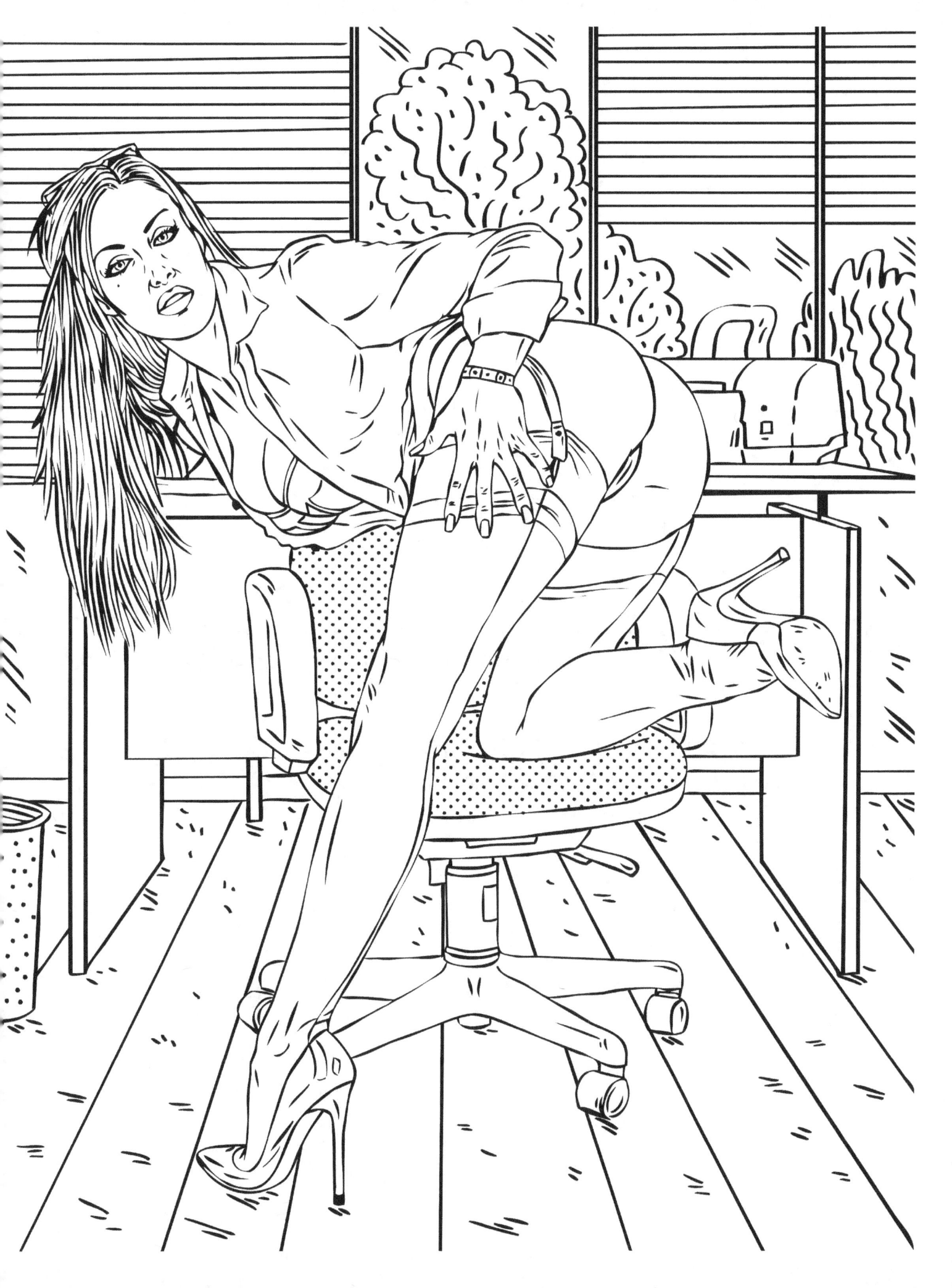

Amanda.
Just looking for the
annual report.

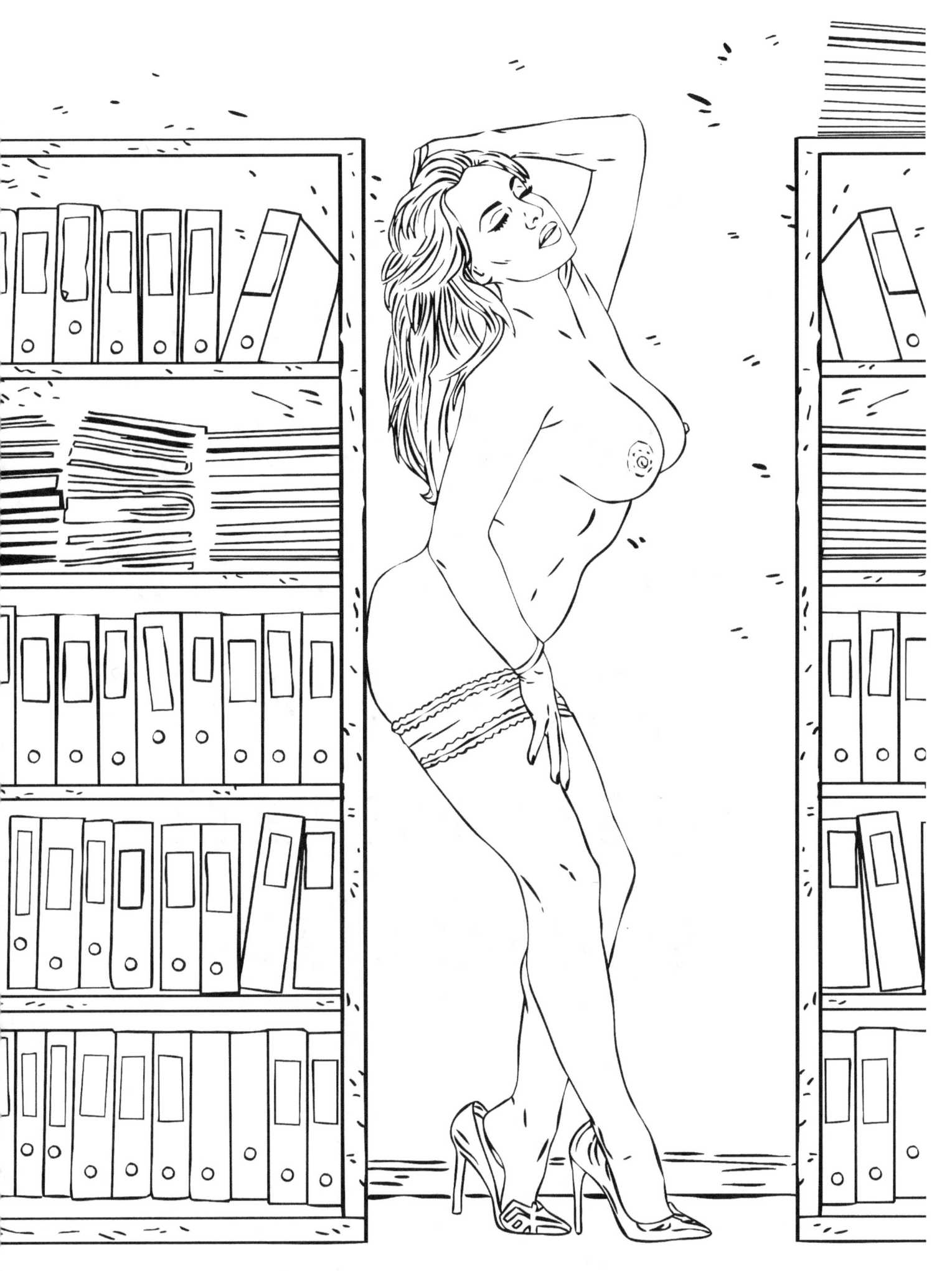

Wanna work with us? You just need to impress our recruitment specialist.

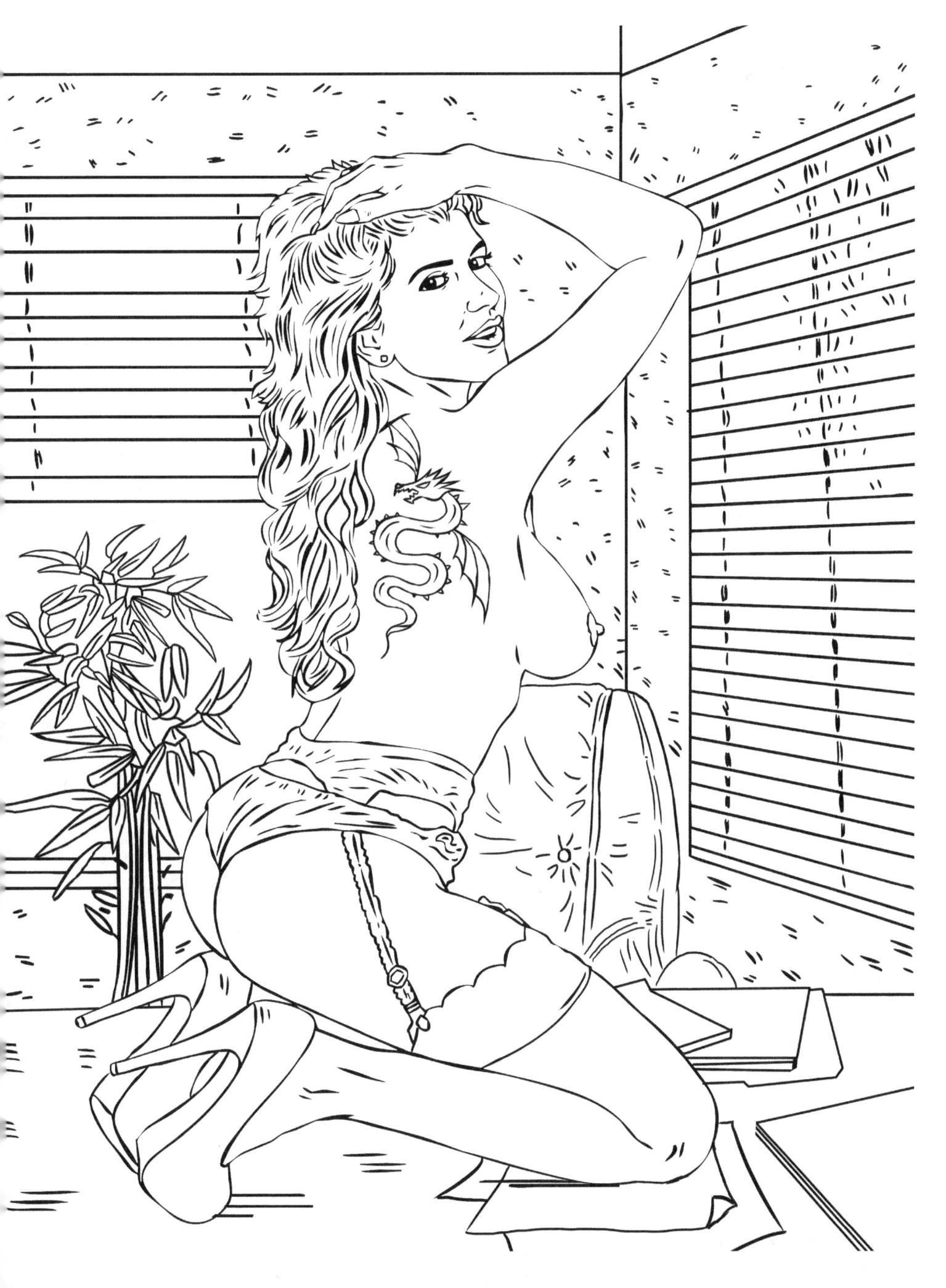

www.ingramcontent.com/pod-product-compliance
Lightning Source LLC
Chambersburg PA
CBHW082021230526
45466CB00022B/2948